PRE-APPRENTICESHIP
MATHS & LITERACY FOR
BUILDING & CARPENTRY
graduated exercises and practice exam

Andrew Spencer

NELSON
A Cengage Company

A+ National Pre-apprenticeship Maths & Literacy for Building & Carpentry
1st Edition
Andrew Spencer

Associate publishing editor: Jana Raus
Project editor: Jana Raus
Senior designer: Vonda Pestana
Text design: Vonda Pestana
Cover design: Ami-Louise Sharpe
Cover image: iStockphoto/Skip ODonnell
Photo research: Libby Henry
Production controller: Alex Ross
Reprint: Alice Kane
Reprint: Magda Koralewska
Reprint: Katie McCappin
Typeset by Macmillan Publishing Services

Any URLs contained in this publication were checked for currency during the production process. Note, however, that the publisher cannot vouch for the ongoing currency of URLs.

Acknowledgements
VCE ® is a registered trademark of the VCAA. The VCAA does not endorse or make any warranties regarding this Cengage product. Current and past VCE Study Designs, VCE exams and related content can be accessed directly at www.vcaa.vic.edu.au

We would like to thank the following for permission to reproduce copyright material:

Corbis Australia: p. 31; Getty Images: p. 13; Photolibrary: pp. 9, 15.

Every effort has been made to trace and acknowledge copyright. However, if any infringement has occurred the publishers tender their apologies and invite the copyright holders to contact them.

For product information and technology assistance,
in Australia call **1300 790 853**;
in New Zealand call **0800 449 725**

For permission to use material from this text or product, please email **aust.permissions@cengage.com**

ISBN 978 0 17 046321 8

Cengage Learning Australia
Level 7, 80 Dorcas Street
South Melbourne, Victoria Australia 3205

Cengage Learning New Zealand
Unit 4B Rosedale Office Park
331 Rosedale Road, Albany, North Shore 0632, NZ

For learning solutions, visit **cengage.com.au**

Printed in Australia by Ligare Pty Limited.
1 2 3 4 5 6 7 25 24 23 22 21

A+ National
PRE-APPRENTICESHIP
Maths & Literacy for Building & Carpentry

Contents

LITERACY	
Unit 1 Spelling	1
Unit 2 Alphabetising	2
Unit 3 Comprehension	3

MATHEMATICS	
Unit 4 General Mathematics	5
Unit 5 Basic Operations	9
Section A: Addition	
Section B: Subtraction	
Section C: Multiplication	
Section D: Division	
Unit 6 Decimals	14
Section A: Addition	
Section B: Subtraction	
Section C: Multiplication	
Section D: Division	
Unit 7 Fractions	19
Section A: Addition	
Section B: Subtraction	
Section C: Multiplication	
Section D: Division	
Unit 8 Percentages	23
Unit 9 Measurement Conversions	25

Introduction

It has always been important to understand, from a teacher's perspective, the nature of the mathematical skills students need for their future, rather than teaching them textbook mathematics. This has been a guiding principle behind the development of the content in this workbook. To teach maths that is *relevant* to students seeking apprenticeships is the best that we can do, to give students an education in the field that they would like to work in.

The content in this resource is aimed at the level that is needed for a student to have the best possibility of improving their maths and literacy skills specifically for trades. Students can use this workbook to prepare for an apprenticeship entry assessment, or even to assist with basic numeracy and literacy at the VET/TAFE level. Coupled with the NelsonNet website, https://www.nelsonnet.com.au/free-resources, these resources have the potential to improve the students' understanding of basic maths concepts that can be applied to trades. These resources have been trialled, and they work.

Commonly used trade terms are introduced so that students have a basic understanding of terminology that they will encounter in the workplace environment. Students who can complete this workbook and reach an 80 per cent or higher outcome in all topics will have achieved the goal of this resource. These students will go on to complete work experience, do a VET accredited course or be able to gain entry into VET/TAFE or an apprenticeship in the trade of their choice.

The content in this workbook is the first step towards bridging the gap between what has been learnt in previous years, and what needs to be remembered and re-learnt for use in trades. Students will significantly benefit from the consolidation of the basic maths and literacy concepts.

Every school has students who want to work with their hands, and not all students want to go to university. The best students want to learn what they do not know; and if students want to learn, this book has the potential to give them a good start in life.

This resource has been specifically tailored to prepare students for sitting apprenticeship or VET/TAFE admission tests, and for giving students the basic skills they will need for a career in trade. In many ways, it is a win–win situation, with students enjoying and studying relevant maths for trades and Registered Training Organisations (RTOs) receiving students that have improved basic maths and literacy skills.

All that is needed is patience, hard work, a positive attitude, a belief in yourself that you can do it and a desire to achieve. The rest is up to you.

About the author

Andrew Spencer has studied education within both Australia and overseas. He has a Bachelor of Education, as well as a Masters of Science in which he specialised in teacher education. Andrew has extensive experience in teaching secondary mathematics throughout New South Wales and South Australia for well over fifteen years. He has taught a range of subject areas, including Maths, English, Science, Classics, Physical Education and Technical Studies. His sense of the importance of practical mathematics has continued to develop with the range of subject areas he has taught in.

Acknowledgements

For Paula, Zach, Katelyn, Mum and Dad.

Many thanks to Mal Aubrey (GTA) and all training organisations for their input.

Thanks also to the De La Salle Brothers for their selfless support and ongoing work with all students.

To Dr Pauline Carter for her unwavering support of all Maths teachers.

This is for all students who value learning, who are willing to work hard and who have character . . . and are characters!

Unit 1: Spelling

Short-answer questions

Specific instructions to students

- This exercise will help you to identify and correct spelling errors.
- Read the following question and then answer accordingly.

Read the following passage and identify and correct the spelling errors.

A carpenter arrives on a buillding site at 7.00 a.m. He brings with him everything that he needs for the eight hours of work ahead. The roof needs replasing as well as the beems on the purgla. In addision, the rufters need cheking, the ladder needs setting up and his tool belt needs to be fetched from his work van. The site managor wants the job completed by noon. The aprentice places all of the tools near the site and then uses the tape to begin measureing the job.

At lunch, the carpenter tells the aprentise that a damiged door has to be removed, repared and replased. The apprentise needs to unscrew the hinges with a Phillips-head scew drver. The job also recquires the door to be varnashed and the window has to be taken out of it. Several deep skratches are in the door and it needs cutting back. There was so much work to do that the bottom line was that the work would not be able to be complated by the end of the day.

Incorrect words:

Correct words:

Unit 2: Alphabetising

Specific instructions to students

- In this unit, you will be able to practise your alphabetising skills.
- Read the following question and then answer the question accordingly.

Put the following words into alphabetical order.

Nail gun	Measuring tape
Generator	Overalls
Ladder	Compressor
Rafters	Hammer
Hammer drill	Saw
Drill bits	Drop saw
Chisel	Angle grinder

_____

_____

_____

_____

_____

_____

_____

_____

_____

_____

_____

_____

_____

_____

Short-answer questions

Specific instructions to students

- This exercise will help you understand what you read.
- Read the following passage and then answer the questions that follow.

Read the following passage and answer the questions in sentence form.

Justin the Carpenter had to be ready to begin work at 6.30 a.m. on Friday. He arrived at 6.15 a.m. and he knew that the he needed to have most of the work completed by 3.15 p.m. The new apprentice, Joe, arrived at 7.00 a.m. and they both began on the largest job. As Justin knew, the weather would be a major consideration because if it rained, all work would have to cease. The rain would make climbing ladders and working on the roofs difficult and, most importantly, unsafe. Joe climbed the ladder and took with him the nail gun, a claw hammer and 250 roofing nails.

In the meantime, Justin collected some pine off of the stack that was delivered the day before. He passed Joe four beams and Joe got to work preparing to fit them in place. As he lifted the first beam, Joe felt a pain in his back and he described it as 'like getting stabbed in the back'. Joe stopped work immediately. Justin told him to climb down and they swapped their positions. Justin continued working on the rafters while Joe rested. Justin worked quickly as the clouds gathered above them. Joe's back recovered after a short rest and he started to pass the beams to Justin.

At 10.00 a.m. they both took a break to have a drink and something to eat. They were on schedule and things looked good. At 10.25 a.m. Justin and Joe resumed work. They worked quickly and constructively and got most of the east side of the house completed. Lunch was at noon and they headed to the local deli to buy something to eat.

They finished lunch at 12.45 p.m. and Justin and Joe began on the west side of the roof. By 1.30 p.m. they were still working very productively, and the roof was looking great. Just then, down came the rain. The working day was over at 1.45 p.m. They had no choice but to pack up and go home.

QUESTION 1

Why would rain cause problems on the work site?

Answer:

QUESTION 2

What tools and equipment did Joe take on to the roof with him?

Answer:

_____

QUESTION 3

Why did Joe have to stop work?

Answer:

_____

QUESTION 4

What time did Justin initially want to finish? What time did he actually finish?

Answer:

_____

QUESTION 5

How long was the working day?

Answer:

_____

MATHEMATICS

Unit 4: General Mathematics

Short-answer questions

Specific instructions to students

- This unit will help you to improve your general mathematical skills.
- Read the questions below and answer all of them in the spaces provided.
- No calculators.
- You will need to show all working.

QUESTION 1

What unit of measurement would you use to measure:

a the length of the top of an oak table?

Answer:

_____

b the temperature of radiator coolant in a van?

Answer:

_____

c the amount of glue in a hot glue gun?

Answer:

_____

d the weight of a roof rafter?

Answer:

_____

e the speed of a vehicle?

Answer:

_____

f the amount of epoxy resin in a container?

Answer:

_____

g the cost of a hammer drill?

Answer:

_____

QUESTION 2

Give examples of how the following might be used in the building industry.

a percentages

Answer:

_____

b decimals

Answer:

_____

c fractions

Answer:

_____

d mixed numbers

Answer:

_____

_____

e ratios

Answer:

_____

f angles

Answer:

_____

QUESTION 3
Convert the following units.

a   1.2 m to centimetres and millimetres

Answer:

___

b   4 tonnes to kilograms

Answer:

___

c   260 cm to millimetres

Answer:

___

d   1140 mL to litres

Answer:

___

e   1650 g to kilograms

Answer:

___

f   1.8 kg to grams

Answer:

___

g   3 m to centimetres and millimetres

Answer:

___

h   4.5 L to millilitres

Answer:

___

QUESTION 4
Write the following in descending order:

0.4   0.04   4.1   40.0   400.00   4.0

Answer:

___

QUESTION 5
Write the decimal number that is between:

a   0.2 and 0.4

Answer:

___

b   1.8 and 1.9

Answer:

___

c   12.4 and 12.5

Answer:

___

d   28.3 and 28.4

Answer:

___

e   101.5 and 101.7

Answer:

___

QUESTION 6
Round off the following numbers to two (2) decimal places.

a   12.346

Answer:

___

b   2.251

Answer:

___

c   123.897

Answer:

___

d   688.882

Answer:

___

e   1209.741

Answer:

___

Estimate the following by approximation.

a   1288 × 19 =

Answer:

b   201 × 20 =

Answer:

c   497 × 12.2 =

Answer:

d   1008 × 10.3 =

Answer:

e   399 × 22 =

Answer:

f   201 − 19 =

Answer:

g   502 − 61 =

Answer:

h   1003 − 49 =

Answer:

i   10 001 − 199 =

Answer:

j   99.99 − 39.8 =

Answer:

What do the following add up to?

a $4, $4.99 and $144.95

Answer:

b   8.75, 6.9 and 12.55

Answer:

c   650 mm, 1800 mm and 2290 mm

Answer:

d   21.3 mm, 119.8 mm and 884.6 mm

Answer:

Subtract the following.

a   2338 from 7117

Answer:

b   1786 from 3112

Answer:

c   5979 from 8014

Answer:

d   11 989 from 26 221

Answer:

e   108 767 from 231 111

Answer:

QUESTION 10

Use division to solve the following.

a $2177 \div 7$

Answer:

---

b $4484 \div 4$

Answer:

---

c $63.9 \div 0.3$

Answer:

---

d $121.63 \div 1.2$

Answer:

---

e $466.88 \div 0.8.$

Answer:

The following information is provided for Question 11.

To solve using BODMAS, in order from left to right, solve the Brackets first, then Of, then Division, then Multiplication, then Addition and lastly Subtraction. The following example has been done for your reference.

EXAMPLE

Solve $(4 \times 7) \times 2 + 6 - 4$.

STEP 1

Solve the Brackets first: $(4 \times 7) = 28$

STEP 2

No Division, so next solve Multiplication: $28 \times 2 = 56$

STEP 3

Addition is next: $56 + 6 = 62$

STEP 4

Subtraction is the last process: $62 - 4 = 58$

FINAL ANSWER:

58

QUESTION 11

Using BODMAS, solve:

a $(6 \times 9) \times 5 + 7 - 2$

Answer:

---

b $(9 \times 8) \times 4 + 6 - 1$

Answer:

---

c $3 \times (5 \times 7) + 11 - 8$

Answer:

---

d $6 + 9 - 5 \times (8 \times 3)$

Answer:

---

e $9 - 7 + 6 \times 3 + (9 \times 6)$

Answer:

---

f $6 + 9 \times 4 + (6 \times 7) - 21$

Answer:

  9780170463218

Unit 5: Basic Operations

Section A: Addition

Short-answer questions

Specific instructions to students

- This section will help you to improve your addition skills for basic operations.
- Read the following questions and answer all of them in the spaces provided.
- No calculators.
- You will need to show all working.

QUESTION 1

A carpenter uses four planks of oak measuring 2 m, 1 m, 3 m and 5 m of 75 mm × 25 mm. How much wood does he use in total?

Answer:

QUESTION 2

To renovate a house a carpenter uses four lengths of pine that measure 2.5 m, 1.8 m, 3.3 m and 15.2 m. How much wood does she use in total?

Answer:

QUESTION 3

A hardware store stocks 2170 of 10 cm galvanised nails, 368 of 8 cm galvanised nails and 723 various galvanised nails. How many nails do they have in stock in total?

Answer:

QUESTION 4

Over four weeks, a carpenter travels 282 km, 344 km, 489 km and 111 km respectively. How far has the carpenter travelled in total over the four weeks?

Answer:

QUESTION 5

A builder uses the following amounts of pine over a month: 32 m in week 1; 47 m in week 2; 57 m in week 3; and 59 m in week 4. How much pine has been used in total?

Answer:

QUESTION 6

An apprentice carpenter buys a hammer for $22, 4 screwdrivers for $16 and a tape measure for $9. How much has been spent in total?

Answer:

QUESTION 7

A carpenter uses 8 cm galvanised nails to complete three jobs on a building site: 86 are used on one job, 132 on another and 97 on the last job. How many have been used in total?

Answer:

QUESTION 8

A woodworker buys a lathe for $1589, a drill for $169 and a circular saw for $209. How much has been spent in total?

Answer:

QUESTION 9

The floors of a restaurant that is being renovated need new timber to replace floorboards that are worn. If 16 m are used for one room, 18 m for another, 8 m for another and 11 m for the last room, how much timber has been used in total?

Answer:

_____

QUESTION 10

To complete some carpentry work, 178 galvanised nails, 188 tacks and 93 wood screws are needed. How many fixers in total are used?

Answer:

_____

Section B: Subtraction

Short-answer questions

Specific instructions to students

- This section will help you to improve your addition skills for basic operations.
- Read the following questions and answer all of them in the spaces provided.
- No calculators.
- You will need to show all working.

QUESTION 1

An apprentice's car is filled to the limit with 52 L of petrol on Wednesday (pay day). If 12 L are used on Friday, 13 L are used on Saturday and 11 L are used on Sunday, how much petrol remains in the tank for work on Monday?

Answer:

_____

QUESTION 2

A cabinet maker has a pack of 500 wood screws. If 244 screws are used in November and 137 screws are used during December, how many screws are left for use in January?

Answer:

_____

QUESTION 3

If Apprentice Carpenter 1 uses 243 m of pine on several jobs and Apprentice Carpenter 2 uses 159 m of pine on different jobs, how much more pine has Apprentice Carpenter 1 used than Apprentice Carpenter 2?

Answer:

_____

_____

QUESTION 4

If a trade assistant uses 72 wood screws from a box that has 250 screws to begin with, how many screws are left?

Answer:

_____

QUESTION 5

It costs $230 to make a cabinet. The boss gives a discount of $27. How much does the customer need to pay?

Answer:

_____

QUESTION 6

A wood yard manager orders 5000 m of pine. Over 6 months, 2756 m of the pine is sold. How much timber remains?

Answer:

_____

9780170463218

QUESTION 7

The area of a storeroom totals 96 m². If 44 m² are used to store timber and 17 m² are used to store tools, how much room, in square metres, remains?

Answer:

QUESTION 8

A builder replaces 69 drill bits over a year. If the builder had a total of 105 drill bits to begin with, how many are now left?

Answer:

QUESTION 9

The odometer of a furniture van reads 56 089 km at the start of the year. At the end of the year, it reads 71 101 km. How many kilometres have been travelled?

Answer:

QUESTION 10

A construction worker uses 31 roofing screws on one job, 29 roofing screws on another job and 103 roofing screws on the last job. If there were 250 screws to begin with, how many screws are now left?

Answer:

Section C: Multiplication

Short-answer questions

Specific instructions to students

- This section will help you to improve your multiplication skills for basic operations.
- Read the following questions and answer all of them in the spaces provided.
- No calculators.
- You will need to show all working.

QUESTION 1

A master builder charges $40 per hour. How much does he earn for a 45-hour week?

Answer:

QUESTION 2

If a cabinet maker uses 14 wood screws to construct a cabinet, how many would be needed to construct 15 more identical cabinets?

Answer:

QUESTION 3

A builder uses 13 L of diesel for one trip to a work site. How much fuel is used if the builder works on the site for 18 days and does the same trip each day?

Answer:

QUESTION 4

A builder uses 12 nuts, 12 bolts and 24 washers on one job. How many nuts, bolts and washers would be used on 24 more identical jobs?

Answer:

QUESTION 5

A carpenter uses 1.5 m of oak for one job, 2.2 m of oak for another job and 0.8 m of oak for the last job. How many metres of oak would be used for 39 more identical jobs?

Answer:

QUESTION 6

To secure four legs on to a table, 16 nuts are used. How many nuts would you need to secure the legs onto 87 more identical tables?

Answer:

QUESTION 7

A tradesman's car uses 9 L of LPG for every 100 km travelled. How much LPG would be used to travel 450 km?

Answer:

QUESTION 8

If a cabinet maker used 673 wood screws per month, how many would be used over one year?

Answer:

QUESTION 9

If a woodworker at a factory uses 8 m of pine each day, how much is used during a month of 31 days?

Answer:

QUESTION 10

If a car travels at 110 km/h for 5 hours, how far will it travel?

Answer:

Section D: Division

Short-answer questions

Specific instructions to students

- This section will help you to improve your division skills for basic operations.
- Read the following questions and answer all of them in the spaces provided.
- No calculators.
- You will need to show all working.

QUESTION 1

A builder has 24 m of pine delivered. How many jobs can be completed if each standard job requires 3 m of pine?

Answer:

QUESTION 2

A cabinet maker earns $868 for working a 5-day week. How much is earned on average per day?

Answer:

9780170463218

QUESTION 3

A carpenter buys 140 L of wood varnish in bulk before pouring it into 4 L containers.

a How many containers will be filled?

Answer:

_____

b Will any varnish be left over?

Answer:

_____

QUESTION 4

A furniture delivery truck travels 780 km in a 5-day week. On average, how many kilometres per day have been travelled?

Answer:

_____

QUESTION 5

The total weight of a specially designed oak table is 88 kg. How much load, in kilograms, is on each of the 4 legs?

Answer:

_____

QUESTION 6

A builder uses 2925 m of pine on 7 different jobs. How many metres are used on each job?

Answer:

_____

QUESTION 7

At a yearly stocktake, a storeman at a furniture company counts 2326 wood screws.

a If 100 screws fit into a box, how many boxes of screws are there?

Answer:

_____

b Are any screws left over?

Answer:

_____

QUESTION 8

A carpentry business tops up its supplies by ordering in 408 packets of wood screws. If 6 packets are put in each box for storage, how many boxes will be needed?

Answer:

_____

QUESTION 9

A truck delivers 645 m of pine to a furniture company. The wood is to be used for making table legs.

a If each leg measures 800 mm, how many legs could be made from the pine?

Answer:

_____

b Is any wood left over?

Answer:

_____

QUESTION 10

A building supervisor travels 3890 km over 28 days while inspecting work sites. How many kilometres are travelled each day on average?

Answer:

_____

Unit 6: Decimals

Section A: Addition

Short-answer questions

Specific instructions to students

- This section will help you to improve your addition skills when working with decimals.
- Read the following questions and answer all of them in the spaces provided.
- No calculators.
- You will need to show all working.

QUESTION 1

If you buy 4 sets of screwdrivers for a total of $137.99 and a claw hammer for $22.75, how much will you spend in total?

Answer:

QUESTION 2

An apprentice carpenter buys a drill for $39.95; a set of drill bits for $29.95; several hole-saws for $44.55; and a set of clamps for $19.45. How much has she spent in total?

Answer:

QUESTION 3

Three lengths of dowel measure 29.85 cm, 19.50 cm and 15.65 cm. What is the total length of the dowel?

Answer:

QUESTION 4

One length of pine measures 1105.5 mm and another length measures 988.5 mm. What is the total length of both pieces of pine?

Answer:

QUESTION 5

An apprentice buys the following for work: a clamp for $8.99; a set of hinges for $6.50; a packet of screws for $6.50; and a door lock for $25.99. What is the total cost?

Answer:

QUESTION 6

If a truck driver travels 65.8 km, 36.5 km, 22.7 km and 89.9 km, how far has she travelled in total?

Answer:

QUESTION 7

What is the total length of a screwdriver with a handle measuring 5.5 cm and an end of 7.8 cm?

Answer:

QUESTION 8

Two sheets of medium-density fireboard (MDF) are fitted side by side. If the side of one sheet measures 2420.5 mm and the side of the other sheet measures 3790.5 mm, what is the combined length of both sides?

Answer:

9780170463218

A cabinet maker completes three jobs: $450.80 is charged for the first job; $1130.65 for the second job; and $660.45 for the last job. How much has been charged in total?

Answer:

QUESTION 10

One side of a wine rack has a length of 89.90 cm. What is the distance around the perimeter if all 4 sides are of equal length?

Answer:

Section B: Subtraction

Short-answer questions

Specific instructions to students

- This section will help you to improve your subtraction skills when working with decimals.
- Read the following questions and answer all of them in the spaces provided.
- No calculators.
- You will need to show all working.

QUESTION 1

From a 2 m length of pine, a carpenter cuts two lengths for support structures in a pergola. If the supports measure 388 mm and 295 mm, how much of the original length, in millimetres, remains?

Answer:

QUESTION 2

If a builder uses a circular saw to cut a 225 mm length from a beam that is 1450 mm long, what is the length of the beam after it is cut?

Answer:

QUESTION 3

An apprentice completes a job that costs $789.20. Her boss then gives a discount of $75.50. How much is the final cost after the discount?

Answer:

QUESTION 4

An apprentice works for 38 hours and earns a total of $245.60. After receiving his wages, he goes to the petrol station and fills the tank of his car with petrol. If the petrol costs $48.85, how much money does he have left?

Answer:

QUESTION 5

Scaffolding is used to reach an area of the outside of a house that is 3.60 m high. The scaffolding then needs to be lowered to a height of 2.95 m to work on the next section of the house. How far down does it need to be lowered?

Answer:

QUESTION 6

Timber is delivered to a building site. Two lengths need to be cut from a 6 m length. The two lengths measure 2250 mm and 2870 mm respectively. How much is left from the original 6 m length?

Answer:

_____

QUESTION 7

If two 1550 mm lengths of pine are cut from a 4 m length, how much pine is left?

Answer:

_____

QUESTION 8

A length of timber measures 1250 mm. If a length of 900 mm is cut from it, how much timber remains?

Answer:

_____

QUESTION 9

A builder has a 5 m length of pine. It is used for three different jobs: 1850 mm for job 1; 1650 mm for job 2; and 950 mm for job 3. How much pine is left?

Answer:

_____

QUESTION 10

A cabinet maker has a 2 m length of Australian oak. If 350 mm is used on one job and then 765 mm and 445 mm are used on two other jobs, how much oak is left?

Answer:

_____

Section C: Multiplication

Short-answer questions

Specific instructions to students

- This section will help you to improve your multiplication skills when working with decimals.
- Read the following questions and answer all of them in the spaces provided.
- No calculators.
- You will need to show all working.

QUESTION 1

A 4 L can of varnish costs $19.95. To complete a job, a cabinet maker needs 5 cans of the varnish. How much will the varnish cost in total?

Answer:

_____

QUESTION 2

One litre of varnish costs $5.50. If an apprentice purchases 16 L of varnish, what is the total cost?

Answer:

_____

9780170463218

QUESTION 3

A cabinet maker replaces 6 pairs of cupboard doors at a cost of $64.50 each. What is the total cost of the replacement doors?

Answer:

QUESTION 4

If a builder uses 6 packets of wood screws that cost $8.65 per packet, how much do the screws cost in total?

Answer:

QUESTION 5

An apprentice buys 12 dyna bolts that cost $1.95 each. How much do the bolts cost in total?

Answer:

QUESTION 6

A master builder earns $43.50 per hour. If he works 50 hours in one week, what is his gross wage (before tax)?

Answer:

QUESTION 7

A furniture workshop buys wood for $2.55 per metre. If 25 m are purchased, how much was spent in total?

Answer:

QUESTION 8

A builder's car has a 52 L tank. Fuel costs $1.95 per litre. How much would the builder have to pay to fill the tank?

Answer:

QUESTION 9

A company manager purchases 3400 m of pine for $2.15 per metre. What is the total outlay?

Answer:

QUESTION 10

A carpenter earns $220.65 per day. What is her gross weekly wage (before tax) for 5 days?

Answer:

Section D: Division

Short-answer questions

Specific instructions to students

- This section will help you to improve your division skills when working with decimals.
- Read the following questions and answer all of them in the spaces provided.
- No calculators.
- You will need to show all working.

QUESTION 1

An apprentice has 28.5 L of varnish that is to be used on 6 separate jobs. How much needs to be allocated for each job if each job needs the same amount of varnish?

Answer:

QUESTION 2

A cabinet maker earns $990.60 for 5 days of work. How much is earned per day?

Answer:

QUESTION 3

A builder charges $3732.70 to complete some work on a house. If it takes 70 hours to complete the job, what is the hourly rate?

Answer:

QUESTION 4

A carpenter completes a job worth $540.85 that takes 16 hours. What is the hourly rate?

Answer:

QUESTION 5

A semitrailer carrying furniture from a warehouse drives from Adelaide to Darwin and travels 3368 km over 5 days. How far has been travelled, on average, each day?

Answer:

QUESTION 6

A carpenter subcontracts a job out to one of his mates. He needs to drive from Adelaide to Melbourne and travels 889.95 km to reach the job. The trip takes 9 hours of driving time. How far has been travelled, on average, per hour?

Answer:

QUESTION 7

A car uses 36 L to travel 575.8 km. How far does the car travel per litre?

Answer:

QUESTION 8

A woodworking workshop buys 36 spanner sets at a cost of $890. How much does one set cost?

Answer:

QUESTION 9

It costs $85.80 to fill a 52 L fuel tank. How much is the cost of fuel per litre?

Answer:

QUESTION 10

A carpenter buys 3 different types of tape measures, totaling $18.60. How much does each tape measure cost if they are the same unit price?

Answer:

9780170463218

Section A: Addition

Short-answer questions

Specific instructions to students

- This section is designed to help you to improve your addition skills when working with fractions.
- Read the following questions and answer all of them in the spaces provided.
- No calculators.
- You will need to show all working.

QUESTION 1

$\frac{1}{2} + \frac{4}{5} =$

Answer:

QUESTION 2

$2\frac{2}{4} + 1\frac{2}{3} =$

Answer:

QUESTION 3

A carpenter pours $\frac{1}{3}$ of a bottle of PVC glue into a container. Another $\frac{1}{4}$ of a bottle of PVC glue is added from another bottle. How much glue is there now in the container in total? Express your answer as a fraction.

Answer:

QUESTION 4

One can of varnish $\frac{1}{3}$ full. Another can is $\frac{1}{2}$ full. How much varnish is there in total? Express your answer as a fraction.

Answer:

QUESTION 5

A cabinet maker has $1\frac{2}{3}$ cans of varnish. $1\frac{1}{4}$ of another can of varnish is added. How much varnish is there in total? Express your answer as a fraction.

Answer:

Section B: Subtraction

Short-answer questions

Specific instructions to students

- This section is designed to help you to improve your subtraction skills when working with fractions.
- Read the following questions and answer all of them in the spaces provided.
- No calculators.
- You will need to show all working.

QUESTION 1

$\frac{2}{3} - \frac{1}{4} =$

Answer:

QUESTION 2

$2\frac{2}{3} - 1\frac{1}{4} =$

Answer:

QUESTION 3

A carpenter has a can of wood varnish that is $\frac{2}{3}$ full. $\frac{1}{2}$ of the can is used as a finish on a dining table. How much varnish is left? Express your answer as a fraction.

Answer:

QUESTION 4

A wood machinist uses oil on two lathes. If there is $\frac{3}{4}$ of a can to begin with, which then is $\frac{1}{3}$ used up, what fraction of oil is left?

Answer:

QUESTION 5

A builder has $2\frac{1}{2}$ containers of PVC glue. If $1\frac{1}{3}$ containers are used for one job, how much glue is left as a fraction?

Answer:

Section C: Multiplication

QUESTION 1

$\frac{2}{4} \times \frac{2}{3} =$

Answer:

QUESTION 2

$2\frac{2}{3} \times 1\frac{1}{2} =$

Answer:

QUESTION 3

A carpenter wants to build a flight of stairs that will have 15 steps in it. What is the total vertical height from the floor to the top of the staircase if each step is $16\frac{1}{2}$ cm high?

Answer:

QUESTION 4

A builder has an $8\frac{1}{2}$ m beam that needs to be cut to $\frac{3}{4}$ of its length. What will the new length measure?

Answer:

QUESTION 5

An apprentice needs to build a 13-step flight of stairs. The height of each step measures $18\frac{1}{2}$ cm. What will be the total vertical height from the floor to the top?

Answer:

Section D: Division

Short-answer questions

Specific instructions to students

- This section is designed to help you to improve your division skills when working with fractions.
- Read the following questions and answer all of them in the spaces provided.
- No calculators.
- You will need to show all working.

QUESTION 1

$\frac{2}{3} \div \frac{1}{4} =$

Answer:

QUESTION 2

$2\frac{3}{4} \div 1\frac{1}{3} =$

Answer:

QUESTION 3

A carpenter has to put new floorboards in a room that is $3\frac{1}{2}$ m wide. How many floorboards will need to be cut, if each floorboard measures 25 cm? (Remember to convert from centimetres into metres.)

Answer:

QUESTION 4

The vertical height of a staircase measures $2\frac{3}{4}$ m. What is the height of each step if 16 steps are required for the staircase?

Answer:

QUESTION 5

A carpenter wants to fit wall panelling across a wall that measures $2\frac{1}{2}$ m. If each panel measures 250 mm, how many are needed? (Hint: Convert the measurement of each panel into centimetres, and then convert it into a fraction of a metre.)

Answer:

Unit 8: Percentages

> **10% rule: Move the decimal one place to the left to get 10%.**

EXAMPLE

10% of $45.00 would be $4.50.

QUESTION 1

A builder repairs a floor at a cost of $5220.00. The builder then gives his client a discount of 10%.

a   How much does the discount work out to in dollars?

Answer:

_____

b   What is the final cost to the client?

Answer:

_____

QUESTION 2

A nail gun costs $249.00 at a hardware shop. The shop then has a sale, and the nail gun is given a 10% discount.

a   How much does the discount work out to in dollars?

Answer:

_____

b   What will the final price of the nail gun be after the 10% is taken off?

Answer:

_____

QUESTION 3

The manager of a woodwork workshop sees a 2 hp air conditioner on sale for $698.00. After negotiating with a sales assistant, a 10% discount is given. How much will the air conditioner cost? (Hint: Find 10% and subtract it from the cost of the air conditioner.)

Answer:

_____

QUESTION 4

A carpenter buys 5 L of thinners for $24.60. He gets a 5% discount. How much does this reduce the price? What is the final price? (Hint: Find 10%, halve it and then subtract it from $24.60.)

Answer:

_____

QUESTION 5

A trade assistant buys 3 packets of sandpaper that add up to $20, a 14 V cordless drill for $69 and 2 sanding blocks that come to $10.50.

a   How much is paid in total?

Answer:

_____

b   How much is paid after a 10% discount?

Answer:

_____

QUESTION 6

The following items are purchased for a woodwork workshop: a fluorescent work light for $19.99; a sanding disc for $9.99, a set of chisels for $89.99, a packet of marking pencils for $6.99 and a 15 m extension lead for $14.99.

a   What is the total cost of all the items?

Answer:

b   What is the final cost after a 10% discount?

Answer:

QUESTION 7

A hardware store offers 20% off of the price of screwdriver sets. If a set is priced at $26 before the discount, how much will they cost after the discount?

Answer:

QUESTION 8

Cordless drills are discounted by 15%. If the regular retail price is $65.00 each, what is the discounted price?

Answer:

QUESTION 9

The regular retail price of a set of chisels is $56.00. If the store has a 20% sale of all items, how much will the chisel set cost during the sale?

Answer:

QUESTION 10

A 1200 amp jump-starter retails for $99. How much will it cost after the store manager takes 30% off?

Answer:

9780170463218

Unit 9: Measurement Conversions

Short-answer questions

Specific instructions to students

- This unit is designed to help you to both improve your skills and to increase your speed in converting one measurement unit into another.
- Read the following questions and answer all of them in the spaces provided.
- No calculators.
- You will need to show all working.

QUESTION 1

How many millimetres are there in 1 cm?

Answer:

QUESTION 2

How many millimetres are there in 1 m?

Answer:

QUESTION 3

How many centimetres are there in 1 m?

Answer:

QUESTION 4

A length of pine if 2550 mm. How long is it in metres?

Answer:

QUESTION 5

The length of a rafter measures 3650 mm. How long is it in metres?

Answer:

QUESTION 6

The strut of a roof measures 2.6 m. How long will it measure in millimetres?

Answer:

QUESTION 7

Two lengths of pine measure 285 cm and 325 cm. What is the total length, in millimetres, when the two are added?

Answer:

QUESTION 8

A carpenter needs three separate lengths of maple to complete a job. The lengths measure 2.45 m, 3.15 m and 1.85 m. What is the total length in millimetres?

Answer:

QUESTION 9

A builder uses four lengths of Australian oak that measure 2580 mm, 3250 mm, 4200 mm and 4400 mm. How much does this measure in total, in metres?

Answer:

QUESTION 10

An apprentice carpenter has 12 m of pine. From this, 5 lengths are cut: 1850 mm, 1350 mm, 1380 mm, 2100 mm and 2350 mm.

a   How long are the 5 lengths put together? State your answer in metres.

Answer:

b   How much is left from the original piece of pine? State your answer in metres.

Answer:

Section A: Circumference

Short-answer questions

Specific instructions to students

- This section is designed to help you both to improve your skills and to increase your speed in measuring the circumference of a round object.
- Read the following questions and answer all of them in the spaces provided.
- No calculators.
- You will need to show all working.

$$C = \pi \times d$$
where: C = circumference, π = 3.14, d = diameter

EXAMPLE

Find the circumference of a sanding disc with a diameter of 150 mm.

$C = \pi \times d$

Therefore, $C = 3.14 \times 150$

$\qquad = 471$ mm

QUESTION 1

Calculate the circumference of a round table with a diameter of 900 mm.

Answer:

_____

QUESTION 2

Find the circumference of a wooden dish with a diameter of 145 mm.

Answer:

_____

QUESTION 3

Determine the circumference of a hole for a kitchen light with a diameter of 120 mm.

Answer:

_____

QUESTION 4

Find the circumference of the top of a wooden stand with a diameter of 16 cm.

Answer:

_____

QUESTION 5

Calculate the circumference of a round feature with a diameter of 12 cm.

Answer:

_____

QUESTION 6

Find the circumference of a wooden coaster with a diameter of 18 cm.

Answer:

_____

QUESTION 7

Calculate the circumference of a round living room table with a diameter of 130 cm.

Answer:

_____

QUESTION 8

Find the circumference of a circular power saw with a diameter of 24 cm.

Answer:

_____

QUESTION 9

Determine the circumference of a sanding disc with a diameter of 14 cm.

Answer:

_____

QUESTION 10

Find the circumference of an orbital sander with a diameter of 17 cm.

Answer:

_____

Section B: Diameter

Short-answer questions

Specific instructions to students

- This section is designed to help you both to improve your skills and to increase your speed in measuring the diameter of a round object.
- Read the following questions and answer all of them in the spaces provided.
- No calculators.
- You will need to show all working.

$$\text{Diameter (D) of a circle} = \frac{\text{circumference}}{\pi(3.14)}$$

EXAMPLE

Find the diameter of a cooking pot with a circumference of 80 mm.

$$D = \frac{80}{\pi(3.14)} = 25.48 \text{ mm}$$

QUESTION 1

Find the diameter of an orbital sander with a circumference of 24 cm.

Answer:

_____

QUESTION 2

Calculate the diameter of a round table with a circumference of 628 cm.

Answer:

_____

QUESTION 3

Find the diameter of a round hole in a door for a window with a circumference of 200 mm.

Answer:

_____

QUESTION 4

Determine the diameter of a hole made by a hole-saw with a circumference of 130 mm.

Answer:

_____

QUESTION 5

Find the diameter of a bored hole with a circumference of 43 mm.

Answer:

_____

QUESTION 6

Determine the diameter of the top of a round telephone table with a circumference of 84 cm.

Answer:

_____

QUESTION 7

Find the diameter of the bottom of a wooden chess piece with a circumference of 12.4 cm.

Answer:

_____

QUESTION 8

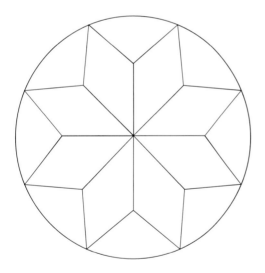

Calculate the diameter of a circular wooden template with a circumference of 90.8 cm.

Answer:

_____

QUESTION 9

Find the diameter of a wooden trivet with a circumference of 62.3 cm.

Answer:

_____

QUESTION 10

Calculate the diameter of a wooden pot plant base with a circumference of 68.8 cm.

Answer:

_____

9780170463218

Section C: Area

> Area = length × breadth and is given in square units
>
> $= l \times b$

QUESTION 1

If the measurements of the base of a trade assistant's tool box are 40 cm long by 21 cm wide, what is the total area?

Answer:

QUESTION 2

A carpenter's workshop measures 60 m by 13 m. What is the workshop's total area?

Answer:

QUESTION 3

If a sheet of plywood measures 2.85 m by 1.65 m, what is its total area?

Answer:

QUESTION 4

The front of a wooden door measures 2.1 m by 0.8 m. What is the door's total area?

Answer:

QUESTION 5

A carpenter purchases a 3 m × 1.5 m sheet of plywood. What is its total surface area?

Answer:

QUESTION 6

The top of a rectangular dining table measures 1.55 m by 1.28 m. What is the total area of the tabletop?

Answer:

QUESTION 7

The measurement of a desktop that a carpenter needs to make is 45 cm by 45 cm. What is the total area of the desktop?

Answer:

QUESTION 8

A storage area for timber is 65.3 m by 32.7 m. How much storage area is available?

Answer:

QUESTION 9

A carpenter's workshop is 8.6 m long by 3.2 m wide. What is its area?

Answer:

QUESTION 10

A van that carries timber measures 8.9 m long and 2.6 m wide. How much floor area is there?

Answer:

Section D: Volume of a cube

> Volume = length × width × height and is given in cubic units
> = *l* × *w* × *h*

QUESTION 1

How many cubic metres are there in a timber yard that has a storage rack that measures 13 m by 5 m by 4 m?

Answer:

QUESTION 2

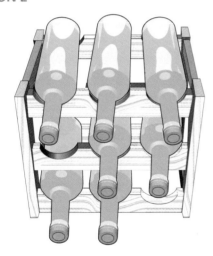

A wine rack is made with the following dimensions: 2 m × 1 m × 0.5 m. What is the wine rack's volume?

Answer:

QUESTION 3

A builder builds a room in a house that measures 3 m long by 2 m high by 3 m wide. How many cubic metres of volume does this make?

Answer:

QUESTION 4

An apprentice constructs a wardrobe that measures 2.2 m × 1.8 m × 0.5 m. How much volume is available inside?

Answer:

QUESTION 5

A carpenter makes a wooden toy box with the dimensions 60 cm by 15 cm by 50 cm. How many cubic centimetres does the toy box contain?

Answer:

QUESTION 6

If a bathroom cabinet measures 1.2 m × 0.6 m × 0.25 m, what cubic area is available for storing bathroom utensils inside it?

Answer:

QUESTION 7

A cabinet maker's toolbox is 50 cm long, 30 cm wide and 25 cm tall. How many cubic centimetres are available for storing tools inside it?

Answer:

QUESTION 8

The boot of a work wagon is 1.4 m wide × 1.6 m long × 88 cm high. What is the volume of the boot? State your answer in cubic centimetres.

Answer:

QUESTION 9

A gyprocker has a storage shed that measures 1.75 m high by 1.35 m wide by 3.6 m long. How many cubic metres of space is there in the shed?

Answer:

QUESTION 10

A carpenter has a room that measures 3.8 m by 3.8 m by 2.5 m. How many cubic metres are there for storage of the carpenter's tools?

Answer:

Section E: Volume of a cylinder

Short-answer questions

Specific instructions to students

- This section is designed to help you both to improve your skills and to increase your speed in calculating the volume of cylinder-shaped objects.
- Read the following questions and answer all of them in the spaces provided.
- No calculators.
- You will need to show all working.

> **Volume of a cylinder** $(V_c) = \pi\ (3.14) \times r^2$
> $(r^2 = \text{radius} \times \text{radius}) \times \text{height}$
> $V_c = \pi \times r^2 \times h$

QUESTION 1

What is the volume of a cylindrical concrete post that has a radius of 13 cm and a height of 90 cm?

Answer:

QUESTION 2

What is the volume of a tube of liquid nails that has a radius of 3 cm and height of 25 cm?

Answer:

QUESTION 3

A can of rust remover has a radius of 4 cm and a height of 11 cm. What is its volume?

Answer:

QUESTION 4

A grease gun has a radius of 2.5 cm and a length of 28 cm. How much grease can it hold?

Answer:

QUESTION 5

A can of lubricant has a radius of 2.5 cm and a height of 16.5 cm. What is its volume?

Answer:

QUESTION 6

A carpenter uses a touch-up airgun to complete a finishing task on some woodwork. If the cylinder has a radius of 5 cm and a height of 25 cm, what is the volume?

Answer:

QUESTION 7

A 4 L container of mineral turpentine gets poured into 3 cylinders. Each cylinder has a radius of 4.5 cm and a height of 20 cm.

a   What is the volume of each container?

Answer:

_____

b   What is the volume of all 3 containers in total?

Answer:

_____

c   How much is left in the 4 L container?

Answer:

_____

QUESTION 8

A container of wood putty has a radius of 10.5 cm and a height of 15 cm.

a   What is its volume?

Answer:

_____

b   If you use exactly half on one job, how much is left?

Answer:

_____

QUESTION 9

A can of general purpose thinners has a radius of 11.7 cm and a height of 22.4 cm.

a   What is its volume?

Answer:

_____

b   If you use 750 mL, how much is left?

Answer:

_____

QUESTION 10

An apprentice uses a can of de-greaser that has a radius of 6 cm and a height of 18 cm. What is its volume?

Answer:

_____

Unit 11: Earning Wages

Short-answer questions

Specific instructions to students

- This unit will help you to calculate how much a job is worth, and how long you need to complete the job.
- Read the following questions and answer all of them in the spaces provided.
- No calculators.
- You will need to show all working.

QUESTION 1

A first-year carpentry apprentice earns $250.40 clear (net) per week. How much is earned per year?

Answer:

QUESTION 2

A trade assistant starts work at 7.00 a.m. and stops for a break at 9.30 a.m. for 20 minutes. Lunch is at 1.15 p.m. for 45 minutes and then he works through to 4.00 p.m. How many hours has he worked for, excluding breaks?

Answer:

QUESTION 3

A cabinet maker earns $35.00 an hour and works a 38-hour week. How much is his gross earnings (before tax)?

Answer:

QUESTION 4

Over a week, an apprentice completes 5 jobs. The cost of each job is as follows: $465.80, $2490.50, $556.20, $1560.70 and $990.60. What is the total cost for all of the jobs?

Answer:

QUESTION 5

A builder constructs a rafter that takes 34 minutes, saws 3 lengths of timber that takes 8 minutes, and then uses 4 lengths of timber to construct a doorframe that takes 27 minutes. How much time has been worked in total on this job? State your answer in hours and minutes.

Answer:

QUESTION 6

A house is being renovated and on the first day a carpenter takes 4½ hours removing timber and roof sheets. If the rate of pay is $28.60 per hour, how much will the carpenter earn?

Answer:

QUESTION 7

An apprentice takes 1½ hours to complete replacing a rafter. If the apprentice is getting paid $14.80 per hour, what are his total earnings?

Answer:

A house suffers storm damage and needs repairing. The carpentry crew spends 116 hours working on the house. If they work 8 hours per day, how many days will it take?

Answer:

An apprentice begins work at 7.00 a.m. and works until 3.30 p.m. The morning break lasts for 20 minutes, the lunch break goes for 60 minutes and the afternoon break lasts 20 minutes.

a How much time has been spent on breaks?

Answer:

b How much time has been spent working?

Answer:

The cost of labour on a renovation job is $960.00. The carpenter spends 24 hours on the job. How much is the rate of pay per hour?

Answer:

9780170463218

Unit 12: Squaring Numbers

Section A: Introducing square numbers

Short-answer questions

Specific instructions to students

- This section is designed to help you both to improve your skills and to increase your speed in squaring numbers.
- Read the following questions and answer all of them in the spaces provided.
- No calculators.
- You will need to show all working.

Any number squared is multiplied by itself.

EXAMPLE

4 squared $= 4^2 = 4 \times 4 = 16$

QUESTION 1

$6^2 =$

Answer:

QUESTION 2

$8^2 =$

Answer:

QUESTION 3

$12^2 =$

Answer:

QUESTION 4

$3^2 =$

Answer:

QUESTION 5

$7^2 =$

Answer:

QUESTION 6

$11^2 =$

Answer:

QUESTION 7

$10^2 =$

Answer:

QUESTION 8

$9^2 =$

Answer:

QUESTION 9

$2^2 =$

Answer:

QUESTION 10

$4^2 =$

Answer:

QUESTION 11

$5^2 =$

Answer:

Section B: Applying square numbers to the trade

Worded practical problems

Specific instructions to students

- This section is designed to help you to both improve your skills and to increase your speed in calculating the area of rectangular or square objects. The worded questions make the content relevant to everyday situations.
- Read the following questions and answer all of them in the spaces provided.
- No calculators.
- You will need to show all working.

QUESTION 1

An apprentice sets aside an area to cut timber. The area measures 2.8 m × 2.8 m. What area does it take up in square metres?

Answer:

QUESTION 2

A carpentry workshop has a work area that is 5.2 m × 5.2 m. What is the total area?

Answer:

QUESTION 3

The dimensions of a kitchen are 2.6 m × 2.6 m. What is the total area?

Answer:

QUESTION 4

An apprentice works in an area that is 15 m × 15 m. If there is an area allocated for storage that is 2.4 m × 2.4 m, how much area is left for the apprentice to work in?

Answer:

QUESTION 5

A furniture workshop has a total floor area of 13.8 m × 13.8 m. The workbench area takes up 1.2 m × 1.2 m and the timber storage area is 2.7 m × 2.7 m. How much area is left to work in?

Answer:

QUESTION 6

A cabinet maker has a sheet of MDF that measures 2.4 m × 2.4 m. If 1.65 m × 1.65 m is cut out of it, how much is left?

Answer:

QUESTION 7

An apprentice cuts out a piece of blueboard for a wet area that measures 50 cm × 50 cm from a sheet that is 120 cm × 120 cm. What area is left?

Answer:

A workshop floor measures 28.2 m × 28.2 m. If it costs $9.50 to seal 1 m², how much will it cost to seal the whole floor?

Answer:

_____

_____

QUESTION 9

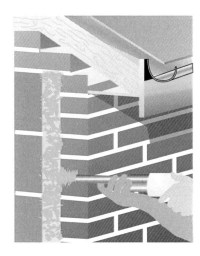

A builder wants to insulate the four walls of a bedroom. Each wall measures 2.6 m × 2.6 m. It costs $28.50 to insulate 1 m².

a How much will it cost to insulate 1 wall?

Answer:

_____

b How much will it cost to insulate all 4 walls?

Answer:

_____

QUESTION 10

A cabinet maker cuts a 1150 mm × 1150 mm piece from a sheet of MDF. What is the total area of the cut piece?

Answer:

_____

Unit 13: Ratios

Section A: Introducing ratios

Short-answer questions

Specific instructions to students

- This section is designed to help to improve your skills in calculating and simplifying ratios.
- Read the following questions and answer all of them in the spaces provided.
- No calculators.
- You will need to show all working.
- Reduce the ratios to the simplest or lowest form.

QUESTION 1

The number of teeth on gear cog 1 is 40. The number of teeth on gear cog 2 is 20. What is the ratio of gear cog 1 to gear cog 2?

Answer:

_____

QUESTION 2

Pulley A has a diameter of 60 cm and pulley B has a diameter of 15 cm. What is the ratio of diameter A to B?

Answer:

_____

QUESTION 3

Pulley belt A has a diameter of 48 cm and pulley belt B has a diameter of 16 cm. What is the ratio of diameter A to B?

Answer:

_____

QUESTION 4

Two gear cogs have 75 and 15 teeth respectively. What is the ratio of the cogs?

Answer:

_____

QUESTION 5

Three cogs have 80 : 60 : 20 teeth respectively. What is the ratio?

Answer:

_____

QUESTION 6

A lathe has 2 pulleys that have diameters of 16 cm and 20 cm respectively. What is the lowest ratio?

Answer:

_____

QUESTION 7

The diameter of pulley A on a band saw is 32 cm. Pulley B has a diameter of 16 cm and pulley C has a diameter of 48 cm. What is the lowest ratio of the three compared together?

Answer:

_____

QUESTION 8

Three pulleys have different diameters: 18 cm, 16 cm and 10 cm respectively. What is the comparative ratio?

Answer:

_____

QUESTION 9

Pulley A has a diameter of 34 cm and pulley B has a diameter of 12 cm. What is the ratio?

Answer:

QUESTION 10

The circumference of pulley A is 62 cm and the circumference of pulley B is 38 cm. What is the ratio?

Answer:

Section B: Applying ratios to the trade

Short-answer questions

Specific instructions to students

- This section is designed to help to improve your practical skills when working with ratios.
- Read the following questions and answer all of them in the spaces provided.
- No calculators.
- You will need to show all working.

QUESTION 1

The ratio of the teeth on cog 1 to cog 2 is 3 : 1. If cog 2 has 10 teeth, how many teeth will cog 1 have?

Answer:

The ratio of the diameter of pulley A to pulley B is 4 : 2. If pulley A has a diameter of 40 cm, what will be the diameter of pulley B?

Answer:

QUESTION 2

The ratio of the teeth on cog 1 to cog 2 is 2 : 1. If cog 2 has 20 teeth, how many teeth will cog 1 have?

Answer:

QUESTION 4

The ratio of the diameter of pulley A to pulley B is 2 : 1. If pulley A has a diameter of 30 cm, what will be the diameter of pulley B?

Answer:

QUESTION 3

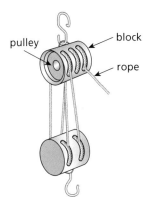

QUESTION 5

The ratio of teeth on cog A to cog B is 3 : 1. If the number of teeth on cog A is 12, how many teeth are on cog B?

Answer:

QUESTION 6

The ratio of teeth on cog A to cog B is 2 : 1. If the number of teeth on cog A is 18, how many teeth are on cog B?

Answer:

QUESTION 7

The ratio of teeth on cog A to cog B is 3 : 1. If the number of teeth on cog A is 21, how many teeth are on cog B?

Answer:

_____

QUESTION 8

The ratio of teeth on cog A to cog B is 3 : 2. If the number of teeth on cog A is 6, how many teeth are on cog B?

Answer:

_____

QUESTION 9

The ratio of teeth on cog A to cog B is 4 : 3. If the number of teeth on cog A is 16, how many teeth will be on cog B?

Answer:

_____

QUESTION 10

The ratio of teeth on cog A to cog B is 4 : 3. If the number of teeth on cog A is 24, how many teeth will be on cog B?

Answer:

_____

9780170463218

Unit 14: Pythagoras' Theorem

Short-answer questions

Specific instructions to students

- This section is designed to help to improve your skills in calculating measurement and area using Pythagoras' theorem.
- Read the following questions and answer all of them in the spaces provided.
- You may use a calculator for this unit to check your answers.
- All working, including approximations, should be done by hand.

The following theorem applies to right-angled triangles, which are often encountered by workers in the building and carpentry industry.

$$a^2 + b^2 = c^2$$

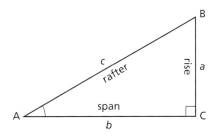

If we consider this formula as it applies to the building trade, we can then introduce the following terms when considering rafters – the main structural roof supports.

a = rise (the change in roof elevation)

b = span (the horizontal distance between the rafter and the rise)

c = diagonal length of the rafter

To find c, or the length of the rafter, you can use the formula:

$$\text{rise}^2 + \text{span}^2 = \text{rafter}^2$$

To solve for c, you need to find the square root of the rise^2 + span^2.

To solve Questions 1–3, you will need to refer to the following example.

If the rise measures 2 m and the span is 4 m, what is the diagonal length of the rafter (c)?

$$\text{rise}^2 + \text{span}^2 = \text{rafter}^2$$
$$2^2 + 4^2 = c^2$$
$$4 + 16 = c^2$$
$$20 = c^2$$
$$\sqrt{20} = c$$
$$4.47 = c$$

Therefore, c, the diagonal length of the rafter or roof, is 4.47 m.

QUESTION 1

If the rise is 3 m and the span is 3 m, what is the diagonal length of the rafter?

Answer:

QUESTION 2

If the rise is 2.1 m and the span is 2.5 m, what is the diagonal length of the rafter?

Answer:

QUESTION 3

If the rise is 2.5 m and the span 4 m, what is the diagonal length of the rafter?

Answer:

To solve Questions 4–6, you will need to refer to the following example.

EXAMPLE

If you know the rise and the diagonal length of the rafter but need to calculate its span, you can subtract the rise squared from the square of the diagonal length of the rafter:

$$span^2 = \text{diagonal length of the rafter}^2 - rise^2$$

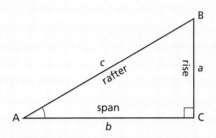

If the diagonal length of the rafter is 5 m and the rise is 2 m, what is the span?

$$span^2 = rafter^2 - rise^2$$
$$span^2 = 5^2 - 2^2$$
$$span^2 = 25 - 4$$
$$span^2 = 21$$
$$span = \sqrt{21}$$
$$span = 4.58$$

Therefore, the span is 4.58 m long.

QUESTION 4

If the diagonal length of the rafter is 4 m and the rise is 3 m, what length is the span?

Answer:

_____

QUESTION 5

If the diagonal length of the rafter is 3.8 m and the rise is 2.2 m, what length is the span?

Answer:

_____

QUESTION 6

If the diagonal length of the rafter is 3.5 m and the rise 1.5 m, what length is the span?

Answer:

_____

To solve Questions 7–9, you will need to refer to the following example.

EXAMPLE

If you know the span and the diagonal length of the rafter and need to calculate the rise, you can subtract the span squared from the square of the diagonal length of the rafter:

$$rise^2 = \text{diagonal length of the rafter}^2 - span^2$$

If the span is 3 m and the diagonal length of the rafter is 4 m, what is the rise?

$$rise^2 = rafter^2 - span^2$$
$$rise^2 = 4^2 - 3^2$$
$$rise^2 = 16 - 9$$
$$rise^2 = 5$$
$$rise = \sqrt{5}$$
$$rise = 2.23$$

Therefore, the rise is 2.23 m long.

QUESTION 7

If the diagonal length of the rafter is 5 m and the span is 4 m, what is the rise?

Answer:

_____

QUESTION 8

If the diagonal length of the rafter is 8 m and the span is 6 m, what is the rise?

Answer:

_____

QUESTION 9

If the diagonal length of the rafter is 7 m and the span 6 m, what is the rise?

Answer:

_____

9780170463218

Unit 15: Trigonometry in Building

Trigonometry can often be used in building to determine measurements and angles. It is particularly useful when trying to find an unknown length.

Trigonometry can be used in conjunction with Pythagoras' theorem: together, they can solve nearly all problems that a builder will come across when using right-angled triangles.

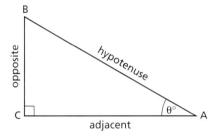

The following rules can be applied to the above triangle.

> **Rule 1**
> $$\sin \theta° = \frac{\text{length of opposite side}}{\text{length of hypotenuse side}} = \frac{\text{opp}}{\text{hyp}}$$
> **Rule 2**
> $$\cos \theta° = \frac{\text{length of adjacent side}}{\text{length of hypotenuse side}} = \frac{\text{adj}}{\text{hyp}}$$
> **Rule 3**
> $$\tan \theta° = \frac{\text{length of opposite side}}{\text{length of adjacent side}} = \frac{\text{opp}}{\text{adj}}$$

The name of each side is determined by the location of the angle in the triangle.

EXAMPLE

If the diagonal length of a rafter is 10 m and the angle that the rafter makes with the span is 27°, find the height of the rise and the length of the span? (Hint: Draw a diagram to illustrate the problem, and then use sin and cos to solve it.)

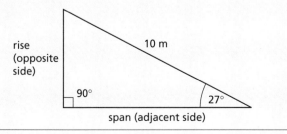

To find the rise:

$\sin 27° = \dfrac{\text{rise}}{10}$

$\sin 27° \times 10 = \text{rise}$

Using a calculator, $\sin 27° = 0.4539$

So $0.4539 \times 10 = 4.54$

Therefore, the height of the rise is 4.54 m.

To find the span:

$\cos 27° = \dfrac{\text{span}}{10}$

$\cos 27° \times 10 = \text{span}$

Using a calculator, $\cos 27° = 0.891$

So, $0.8910 \times 10 = 8.91$

Therefore, the length of the span is 8.91 m.

Solve the following by first drawing a diagram to illustrate each problem and then using sin and cos.

QUESTION 1

If the diagonal length of a roof is 5 m and the angle that the roof makes with the span is 21°, find the height of the rise and the length of the span.

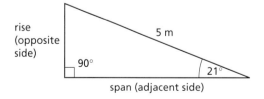

Answer:

_____

QUESTION 2

If the diagonal length of a roof is 8000 mm and the angle that the roof makes with the span is 25°, find the height of the rise and the length of the span.

Answer:

QUESTION 3

If the diagonal length of a rafter is 11 m and the angle that the roof makes with the span is 27°, find the height of the rise and the length of the span.

Answer:

In a rafter construction job, the angle that a rafter makes with the span is 25° on each side. The length of the span is 4 m. Calculate the rise and diagonal length of the rafters on each side of the roof. (Remember to make a right angle in your drawing before you begin.)

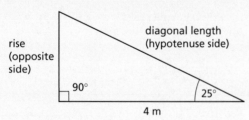

rise (opposite side)

diagonal length (hypotenuse side)

90°

25°

4 m

To find the diagonal length of the rafter:

$$\cos 25° = \frac{4}{\text{diagonal length}}$$
$$\text{diagonal length} = \frac{4}{\cos 25°}$$
$$\text{diagonal length} = \frac{4}{0.9063}$$
$$\text{diagonal length} = 4.41 \text{ m}$$

Therefore, the diagonal length of the rafter is 4.41 m.

To find the rise:

$$\sin 27° = \frac{\text{rise}}{4.41}$$
$$\sin 27° \times 4.41 = \text{rise}$$
$$0.4539 \times 4.41 = \text{rise}$$
$$2 = \text{rise}$$

Therefore, the height of the rise is 2 m.

Solve the following by first drawing a diagram to illustrate each problem and then using sin, cos or tan.

QUESTION 4

If the total length of the span is 4 m and the angle that the rafter makes with the span is 28° on both sides, find the diagonal length of the rafters of the roof and the rise.

Answer:

QUESTION 5

If the total length of the span is 10 m and the angle that the rafter makes with the span is 23° on both sides, find the diagonal length of the rafters and the rise.

Answer:

QUESTION 6

If the total length of the span is 9 m and the angle that the rafter makes with the span is 25° on both sides, find the diagonal length of the rafters and the rise.

Answer:

Unit 16: Mechanical Reasoning

Short-answer questions

Specific instructions to students

- This section is designed to help to improve your skills in mechanical reasoning.
- Read the following questions and answer all of them in the spaces provided.
- No calculators.
- You will need to show all working.

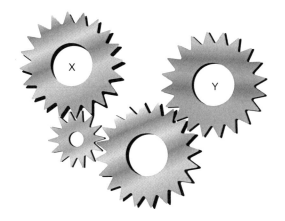

If cog X turns in a clockwise direction, which way will cog Y turn?

Answer:

_____

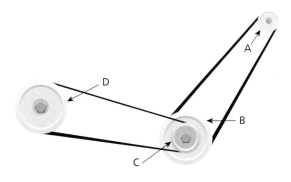

If pulley A turns in a clockwise direction, which way will pulley D turn?

Answer:

_____

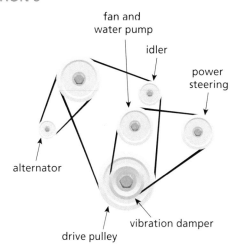

If the drive pulley in a work van engine turns in a clockwise direction, in which direction will the alternator turn?

Answer:

_____

Looking at the following diagram, if lever A moves to the left, in which direction will lever B move?

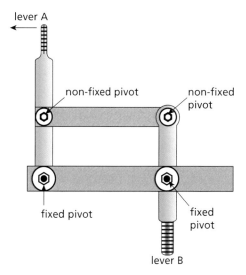

Answer:

_____

In the following diagram, pully 1 turns clockwise. In what direction will pully 6 turn?

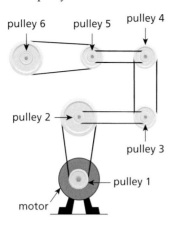

Answer:

_____

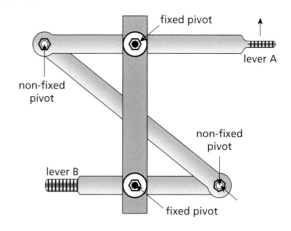

If lever A is pulled up, what will happen to lever B?

Answer:

_____

Building & Carpentry
Practice Written Exam for the Building & Carpentry Trade

Reading time: 10 minutes

Writing time: 1 hour 30 minutes

Section A: Literacy

Section B: General Mathematics

Section C: Trade Mathematics

QUESTION and ANSWER BOOK

Section	Topic	Number of questions	Marks
A	Literacy	7	22
B	General Mathematics	11	24
C	Trade Mathematics	40	54
		Total 58	Total 100

The sections may be completed in the order of your choice.

NO CALCULATORS are to be used during the exam.

Section A: Literacy

Spelling

Read the passage below and then underline the 20 spelling errors.

10 marks

Griffo the Bulder arrived on site at 6.00 a.m. The house is a two-story timbur construktion and the builder has a crew of fore working with him. Shaun headed off to work on the kitchan while Darryl started work in the bathrom. Shaun took eighteen skredrivers with him to assist with asembling the supports. He could complete most of the work by himself. Darryl knew it would not take long to line the bathroom. He knew how to gyprok and he had no problum lifting each sheet into plase.

Upstares, Jane and David were working on the ensweet and soon they had everything looking good. Griffo needed six new drill bits, so he heded for the work van and grabed a new set. It wasn't long before everything was taking shape and Griffo was happy with the crew's work. He desided to give them all a bonuss for the great work that they had completed ahead of schedule.

Correct the spelling errors by writing them out with the correct spelling below.

_____

_____

Alphabetising

Put the following words into alphabetical order.

7 marks

Ladder	Drill
Hammer	Wood screw
Tool belt	Tape measure
Screwdriver	Pine
Coping saw	Mahogany
Circular saw	Router
Set square	Wood glue

_____

_____

_____

_____

_____

_____

_____

9780170463218

_____
_____
_____
_____
_____
_____
_____
_____

Comprehension

Short-answer questions

Specific instructions to students

- Read the passage and then answer the questions that follow.

It was five o'clock in the morning when Daryle received an urgent phone call. During the night, a violent storm had lashed the Central Coast and he was needed immediately to secure the tiles on several houses and ensure that there was no structural damage to the buildings. He rang his mates Tim, Trevor and Herb who he would need to help do the work. Tim had the work van, so he picked up the others and they headed to the Central Coast. The trip took just over two hours and when they arrived, they couldn't believe the destruction that had taken place!

Roofs had come apart, timber and electrical wires were exposed, and the rain had not eased. This was not going to be an easy job. Tim, Trevor and Herb quickly assessed the damage and then prioritised which houses needed attention first. They decided to help an elderly couple who had a tree fall onto their roof, which had left a gaping hole. They removed all of the damaged timber and the tree before lifting four lengths of 5 m pine onto the roof. This timber needed to be made ready to be cut so that it could replace the damaged timber. Tim was used to lifting and easily moved the timber into place. Herb had the most experience, and he could quickly weigh up the extent of damage and how much timber was needed to be replaced. Trevor was good at making tea and coffee and always brought along enough biscuits for everyone.

After five hours, the elderly couple's house was repaired and it was safe to move them back in. The elderly couple was very grateful. Daryle helped them clean their possessions and he helped to settle them back in. In the meantime Tim, Herb and Trevor moved on to the next house, which had two large branches broken off and each was protruding from the side of the house. The three used chainsaws to cut back the branches and then they removed them. This job was going to take significantly longer than the last due to the significant damage that had been caused. All in all, it took the crew of four 14 days to repair all of the damaged houses.

QUESTION 1   1 mark

At what time did Daryle receive the first phone call?

Answer:

_____

QUESTION 2   1 mark

How many people, including Daryle, made up the working crew?

Answer:

_____

QUESTION 3   1 mark

Why was the job not going to be 'easy'?

Answer:

_____

_____

_____

QUESTION 4   1 mark

What were Tim, Herb and Trevor each 'good at', according to the passage?

Answer:

_____

_____

_____

_____

QUESTION 5   3 marks

What did the crew first need to do to the two protruding branches before removing them from the side of the second house?

Answer:

_____

_____

Section B: General Mathematics

QUESTION 1   3 marks

What unit of measurement would you use to measure:

a   a length of timber?

Answer:

_____

b   the roof temperature?

Answer:

_____

c   the amount of wood glue?

Answer:

_____

QUESTION 2   3 marks

Write an example of the following and give an instance where it may be found in the building industry.

a   percentages

Answer:

_____

b   decimals

Answer:

_____

c   fractions

Answer:

_____

QUESTION 3   2 marks

Convert the following units.

a   5 kilograms to grams

Answer:

___

b   7 tonnes to kilograms

Answer:

___

QUESTION 4   2 marks

Write the following in descending order:

0.7   0.71   7.1   70.1   701.00   7.0

Answer:

___

QUESTION 5   2 marks

Write the decimal number that is between:

a   0.1 and 0.2

Answer:

___

b   1.3 and 1.4

Answer:

___

QUESTION 6   2 marks

Round off the following numbers to two (2) decimal places.

a   5.177

Answer:

___

b   12.655

Answer:

___

QUESTION 7   2 marks

Estimate the following by approximation.

a $101 \times 81 =$

Answer:

___

b $399 \times 21 =$

Answer:

___

QUESTION 8   2 marks

What do the following add up to?

a $7, $13.57 and $163.99

Answer:

___

b   4, 5.73 and 229.57

Answer:

___

QUESTION 9   2 marks

Subtract the following.

a   196 from 813

Answer:

___

b   5556 from 9223

Answer:

___

QUESTION 10   2 marks

Use division to solve:

a $4824 \div 3 =$

Answer:

___

b $84.2 \div 0.4 =$

Answer:

___

QUESTION 11　　　　　　　　　　2 marks

Using BODMAS, solve:

a　$(3 \times 7) \times 4 + 9 - 5 =$

Answer:

b　$(8 \times 12) \times 2 + 8 - 4 =$

Answer:

Section C: Trade Mathematics

Basic operations

Addition

QUESTION 1　　　　　　　　　　1 mark

An apprentice carpenter uses 3 m, 16 m, 39 m and 42 m of pine on a building job. How much pine has been used in total?

Answer:

QUESTION 2　　　　　　　　　　1 mark

A builder charges $863 for labour and $2368 for timber while working on a house. How much is the total bill?

Answer:

Subtraction

QUESTION 1　　　　　　　　　　1 mark

A work van is filled up with 36 L of LPG. The tank is now at its maximum of 52 L. A driver uses the following amounts of LPG on each day:

Monday: 5 L

Tuesday: 11 L

Wednesday: 10 L

Thursday: 8 L

Friday: 7 L

How many litres of LPG are left in the tank?

Answer:

QUESTION 2　　　　　　　　　　1 mark

If a cabinet maker has 224 wood screws in stock and 179 are used over 4 weeks, how many are left?

Answer:

Multiplication

QUESTION 1　　　　　　　　　　1 mark

A cabinet maker uses 14 nuts, 24 washers and 14 bolts on a kitchen fix. How many nuts, washers and bolts would be used on 9 similar fixes?

Answer:

QUESTION 2　　　　　　　　　　1 mark

To make a cabinet, a carpenter uses 2 m of Tasmanian oak, 3 m of pine and 1 m of plywood. How much of each would be used to make 12 of these cabinets?

Answer:

Division

A builder has a box of 250 wood screws.

a   How many jobs can be completed if each standard job requires 8 wood screws?

Answer:

b   Would any screws be left over?

Answer:

If an apprentice earns $288.80 for working a 5-day week, how much is earned per day?

Answer:

Decimals

Addition

A set of sockets and a hammer drill are purchased for $27.99 and $156.50 respectively. How much is paid in total?

Answer:

An apprentice carpenter purchases a heat gun kit for $49.95, a 1500 W circular saw for $89.95, a 900 W planer for $95.95 and a 1500 W compound mitre saw for $199.50. How much has been spent in total?

Answer:

Subtraction

A builder has a 4 m length of pine to be used on three different jobs: 1185 mm is used for job 1, 1560 mm on job 2 and 1135 mm on job 3. How much pine is left?

Answer:

A woodworker has a 6 m length of pine. If 2.78 m is used on one job, 1.76 m on another and 1.44 m on the last job, how much is left on the reel?

Answer:

Multiplication

A builder replaces 6 drill bits at a cost of $6.99 each and buys 4 quick grip clamps for $5.99 each. What is the total cost?

Answer:

If an apprentice carpenter uses 6 packets of 50 mm wood screws that cost $9.50 per packet, how much is the total cost?

Answer:

Division

QUESTION 1   1 mark

A carpenter takes 12 hours to complete 3 jobs and the total bill is $582.48. How much does the carpenter charge per hour?

Answer:

_____

QUESTION 2   1 mark

A wood workshop buys 240 pairs of safety glasses in bulk at a total cost of $2160. How much is the cost of one pair?

Answer:

_____

Fractions

QUESTION 1   1 mark

$\frac{2}{3} + \frac{3}{4} =$

Answer:

_____

QUESTION 2   1 mark

$\frac{4}{5} - \frac{1}{3} =$

Answer:

_____

QUESTION 3   1 mark

$\frac{2}{3} \times \frac{1}{4} =$

Answer:

_____

QUESTION 4   1 mark

$\frac{3}{4} \div \frac{1}{2} =$

Answer:

_____

Percentages

QUESTION 1   2 marks

A repair bill on a house comes to $1380.00.

a   How much is 10% of the bill?

Answer:

_____

b   What is the final bill once 10% is taken off?

Answer:

_____

QUESTION 2   2 marks

A carpenter buys a new 600 mm spirit level, a new claw hammer and a new laser-guided handsaw. The total comes to $170.50.

a   What is 10% of the total?

Answer:

_____

b   How much is the final total once the 10% is taken off?

Answer:

_____

Measurement conversions

QUESTION 1   1 mark

How many millimetres are there in 3.85 m?

Answer:

_____

QUESTION 2   1 mark

2285 mm converts into how many metres?

Answer:

_____

Measurement: Length, area and volume

Circumference

QUESTION 1   1 mark

What is the circumference of a circular saw with a diameter of 24 cm?

Answer:

_____

QUESTION 2   1 mark

What is the circumference of an orbital sander with a diameter of 15 cm?

Answer:

_____

Diameter

QUESTION 1   1 mark

What is the diameter of a cut-off saw with a circumference of 115 cm?

Answer:

_____

QUESTION 2   1 mark

What is the diameter of an angle grinder's disc with a circumference of 32 cm?

Answer:

_____

Area

QUESTION 1   1 mark

If a workshop's floor measures 20 m by 21.2 m, what is the total area?

Answer:

_____

QUESTION 2   1 mark

A rectangular length of plywood measures 300 cm long by 150 cm wide. How much area does the rectangular length contain?

Answer:

_____

Volume of a cube

QUESTION 1   1 mark

A small trailer measures 2 m by 2 m by 0.5 m. How much volume can the trailer hold?

Answer:

_____

QUESTION 2   1 mark

The dimensions of a toolbox are 60 cm by 15 cm by 10 cm. What is its total volume?

Answer:

_____

Volume of a cylinder

QUESTION 1   1 mark

A tube of liquid nails has a radius of 3 cm and a length of 30 cm. How much grease can it hold?

Answer:

_____

QUESTION 2   2 marks

A container of wood filler has a radius of 8 cm and a height of 12 cm.

a   What is its volume?

Answer:

_____

b   If you use half on one job, how much is left?

Answer:

_____

Earning wages

QUESTION 1   1 mark

A first-year apprentice carpenter earns $280.60 net (take home) per week. How much does he earn per year? (Note that there are 52 weeks in a year.)

Answer:

_____

QUESTION 2   1 mark

A house has major damage after a storm. The labour bill comes to $2860. If the builder spends 48 hours working on the house, what is the rate for labour per hour?

Answer:

_____

Squaring numbers

QUESTION 1   1 mark

What is 6^2?

Answer:

_____

QUESTION 2   1 mark

A workshop has an area for a wood lathe that is 5.2 m × 2.2 m. What is the total area?

Answer:

_____

Ratios

QUESTION 1   1 mark

A driver cog has 20 teeth and the driven cog has 60 teeth. What is the ratio, in the lowest form, of the driver cog to the driven cog?

Answer:

_____

QUESTION 2   1 mark

The ratio of the diameters of driver pulley A to driven pulley B is 1 : 4. If the diameter of driver pulley A is 15 cm, what is the diameter of driven pulley B?

Answer:

_____

Pythagoras' theorem

QUESTION 1   2 marks

A roof has a rise of 2 m and a span of 4 m. How long are the diagonal sides of the roof? (Hint: draw a diagram before solving to find the answer.)

Answer:

_____

QUESTION 2   2 marks

A roof has a rise of 3 m and a span of 5 m. How long is the diagonal side of the roof? (Hint: draw a diagram before solving to find the answer.)

Answer:

_____

Trigonometry

QUESTION 1 2 marks

The angle that the side of a roof makes with the base of the rafter is 28°. The span is 3 m. Calculate the rise of the roof using trigonometry. (Remember to draw a diagram first.)

Answer:

___

QUESTION 2 2 marks

The angle that the side of a roof makes with the base of the rafter is 21°. The span is 3 m. Calculate the rise of the side of the roof using trigonometry. (Remember to draw a diagram first.)

Answer:

Mechanical reasoning

QUESTION 1 1 mark

Pully 1 and pully 2 each measure 5 cm across their diameters. Pully 3 measures 10 cm across the diameter. How many times will pulleys 1 and 2 turn if pully 3 turns 3 times?

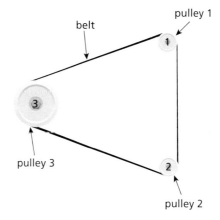

Answer:

___

QUESTION 2 1 mark

Each cog in the below diagram has 16 teeth and they interlock with each other. If cog 5 turns in an anticlockwise direction, which way will cog 1 turn?

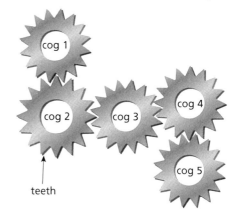

Answer:

___

Glossary

Beam   A term used for joists, girders or rafters

Casing   The trim around a door or window, either outside or inside

Circumference   The perimeter of a circle

Cornice   The exterior trim from the top of the wall to the projection of the rafters

Diameter   A line passing through the centre of a circle, extending from one side of the circumference to the other

Drywall   A wall covering of gypsum board

Fascia   A board that is nailed to the ends of the rafters

Flashing   Any material that is used around chimneys, vents and windows that prevents moisture from entering the building

Flush   Two members that form an even surface

Footing   Enlargement at the base of a column or foundation wall

Foundation   The supporting structure found below grade. It is comprised of the footing with the foundation wall

Gable roof   A roof formed by universal rafters; it slopes up from two walls

Gusset   A bracket or panel that could be made of wood or metal that is attached to the corners of a frame to provide additional strength

Jamb   The vertical posts that make up a window or doorframe

Joint   The place where two or possibly more members come together

Joist   This is a beam that can support a floor or ceiling

Masonry   Mortar bonds with materials to form a wall

Mortise   A hole or slot that a part or tenon may fit into

Particle board   A combination of woodchips and resin binder that are pressed into sheets that vary in thickness

Perimeter   The length of a boundary around a shape

Pitch (roof)   The incline of a roof as found by the rise divided by the span

Radius   The shortest distance from the centre of a circle to the circumference

Rafter   The main structural support of a roof

Ridge   The highest horizontal section of a roof

Rise   The change in elevation of a roof or stairs

Scaffold   A temporary platform that may be used to support both workers and/or equipment

Span   The distance between opposite sides of a building

Formulae and data

Circumference of a Circle

$C = \pi \times d$

where: C = circumference, π = 3.14, d = diameter

Diameter of a Circle

Diameter (d) of a circle $= \dfrac{\text{circumference}}{\pi \,(3.14)}$

Area

Area = length × breadth and is given in square units

$\quad = l \times b$

Volume of a Cube

Volume = length × width × height and is given in cubic units

$\quad = l \times w \times h$

Volume of a Cylinder

Volume of a cylinder (V_c) = π (3.14) × r^2 (r^2 = radius × radius) × height

$V_c = \pi \times r^2 \times h$

Pythagoras' Theorem

$a^2 + b^2 = c^2$

Trigonometry

Rule 1

$\sin \theta^\circ = \dfrac{\text{length of opposite side}}{\text{length of hypotenuse side}} = \dfrac{\text{opp}}{\text{hyp}}$

Rule 2

$\cos \theta^\circ = \dfrac{\text{length of adjacent side}}{\text{length of hypotenuse side}} = \dfrac{\text{adj}}{\text{hyp}}$

Rule 3

$\tan \theta^\circ = \dfrac{\text{length of opposite side}}{\text{length of adjacent side}} = \dfrac{\text{opp}}{\text{adj}}$

Times Tables

1

1 × 1	=	1
2 × 1	=	2
3 × 1	=	3
4 × 1	=	4
5 × 1	=	5
6 × 1	=	6
7 × 1	=	7
8 × 1	=	8
9 × 1	=	9
10 × 1	=	10
11 × 1	=	11
12 × 1	=	12

2

1 × 2	=	2
2 × 2	=	4
3 × 2	=	6
4 × 2	=	8
5 × 2	=	10
6 × 2	=	12
7 × 2	=	14
8 × 2	=	16
9 × 2	=	18
10 × 2	=	20
11 × 2	=	22
12 × 2	=	24

3

1 × 3	=	3
2 × 3	=	6
3 × 3	=	9
4 × 3	=	12
5 × 3	=	15
6 × 3	=	18
7 × 3	=	21
8 × 3	=	24
9 × 3	=	27
10 × 3	=	30
11 × 3	=	33
12 × 3	=	36

4

1 × 4	=	4
2 × 4	=	8
3 × 4	=	12
4 × 4	=	16
5 × 4	=	20
6 × 4	=	24
7 × 4	=	28
8 × 4	=	32
9 × 4	=	36
10 × 4	=	40
11 × 4	=	44
12 × 4	=	48

5

1 × 5	=	5
2 × 5	=	10
3 × 5	=	15
4 × 5	=	20
5 × 5	=	25
6 × 5	=	30
7 × 5	=	35
8 × 5	=	40
9 × 5	=	45
10 × 5	=	50
11 × 5	=	55
12 × 5	=	60

6

1 × 6	=	6
2 × 6	=	12
3 × 6	=	18
4 × 6	=	24
5 × 6	=	30
6 × 6	=	36
7 × 6	=	42
8 × 6	=	48
9 × 6	=	54
10 × 6	=	60
11 × 6	=	66
12 × 6	=	72

7

1 × 7	=	7
2 × 7	=	14
3 × 7	=	21
4 × 7	=	28
5 × 7	=	35
6 × 7	=	42
7 × 7	=	49
8 × 7	=	56
9 × 7	=	63
10 × 7	=	70
11 × 7	=	77
12 × 7	=	84

8

1 × 8	=	8
2 × 8	=	16
3 × 8	=	24
4 × 8	=	32
5 × 8	=	40
6 × 8	=	48
7 × 8	=	56
8 × 8	=	64
9 × 8	=	72
10 × 8	=	80
11 × 8	=	88
12 × 8	=	96

9

1 × 9	=	9
2 × 9	=	18
3 × 9	=	27
4 × 9	=	36
5 × 9	=	45
6 × 9	=	54
7 × 9	=	63
8 × 9	=	72
9 × 9	=	81
10 × 9	=	90
11 × 9	=	99
12 × 9	=	108

10

1 × 10	=	10
2 × 10	=	20
3 × 10	=	30
4 × 10	=	40
5 × 10	=	50
6 × 10	=	60
7 × 10	=	70
8 × 10	=	80
9 × 10	=	90
10 × 10	=	100
11 × 10	=	110
12 × 10	=	120

11

1 × 11	=	11
2 × 11	=	22
3 × 11	=	33
4 × 11	=	44
5 × 11	=	55
6 × 11	=	66
7 × 11	=	77
8 × 11	=	88
9 × 11	=	99
10 × 11	=	110
11 × 11	=	121
12 × 11	=	132

12

1 × 12	=	12
2 × 12	=	24
3 × 12	=	36
4 × 12	=	48
5 × 12	=	60
6 × 12	=	72
7 × 12	=	84
8 × 12	=	96
9 × 12	=	108
10 × 12	=	120
11 × 12	=	132
12 × 12	=	144

9780170463218

Multiplication Grid

×	1	2	3	4	5	6	7	8	9	10	11	12
1	1	2	3	4	5	6	7	8	9	10	11	12
2	2	4	6	8	10	12	14	16	18	20	22	24
3	3	6	9	12	15	18	21	24	27	30	33	36
4	4	8	12	16	20	24	28	32	36	40	44	48
5	5	10	15	20	25	30	35	40	45	50	55	60
6	6	12	18	24	30	36	42	48	54	60	66	72
7	7	14	21	28	35	42	49	56	63	70	77	84
8	8	16	24	32	40	48	56	64	72	80	88	96
9	9	18	27	36	45	54	63	72	81	90	99	108
10	10	20	30	40	50	60	70	80	90	100	110	120
11	11	22	33	44	55	66	77	88	99	110	121	132
12	12	24	36	48	60	72	84	96	108	120	132	144

Notes

Notes

Notes

Notes

Notes